Southern Exposure

Southern Exposure

The Story of Southern Music in Pictures and Words

RICHARD CARLIN ✲ BOB CARLIN

BILLBOARD BOOKS

AN IMPRINT OF WATSON-GUPTILL PUBLICATIONS
New York

Acknowledgments

Thanks to our parents for dragging us to all those folk-music shows; to the many musicians who have played with us and influenced our own understanding and growth; to the many scholars who have come before us and researched this music; to the many collectors who have prized and cherished these images; and to the archivists and librarians who helped us find them. Special thanks to our wives, Rachel Smith and Jessica Myers, for tolerating the many interruptions that musical lives bring. And for Benjamin, who we hope someday will be dragging his children to all those folk-music shows.

Senior Acquisitions Editor: Bob Nirkind
Associate Editor: Alison Hagge
Production Manager: Hector Campbell
Design: Jay Anning, Thumb Print

First published in 2000 by Billboard Books
an imprint of Watson-Guptill Publications
a division of BPI Communications, Inc.
1515 Broadway, New York, NY 10036

Library of Congress Cataloging-in-Publication Data
    Carlin, Richard.
    Southern Exposure : the story of Southern music in pictures and words / by Richard Carlin and Robert Carlin ; with a foreword by John Hartford.
        p.   cm.
    Includes index.
    ISBN 0-8230-8426-4
    1. Folk music—Southern States—History and criticism. 2. Folk musicians—Southern States—Portraits. I. Carlin, Bob. II. Title.
    ML3557.C37 2000
    781.62'13075—dc21   00-021668

The principal typefaces used in the composition of this book were 36 point Caslon Antique and 11 point Adobe Garamond.

Manufactured in the United States of America

First printing, 2000

1 2 3 4 5 6 7 8 9 / 08 07 06 05 04 03 02 01 00

CONTENTS

FOREWORD

THERE'S NOTHING LIKE the feeling of a spring day with the prospect of taking off somewhere in an old car with some other musicians and everyone all cleaned up and flushed with the anticipation of playing for someone, anyone, anywhere. In the old days, that was what it was about. Tuning up on some little bandstand or getting up on the back of a flatbed truck wearing hats and white shirts and ties and, yes, being on the radio once or twice where you feel like a minor celebrity (in your own mind). There was also the feeling of playing music, tinkering with music, or listening to your own special music (or at least what you share with those who are close to you) on a back porch, in a yard, in a kitchen with coffee brewing, with the whole family and circle of extended family creating the most secure, wonderful, sunshiny feeling (especially when it's raining or snowing outside).

My cousin and I used to take our instruments to school and pick during recess and we'd keep them in the office of the school shop, which worked good 'cause the shop teacher was also a square-dance caller and really liked our kind of music. Those instruments that we played—it was very important what they were and what they looked like in addition to what they sounded like. I had a banjo that didn't have enough inlay, so I got a bunch of buttons and just inlaid curlicues all up and down that neck. It would pert near blind you. Also important was how you held them and how you stood. At some point you would get someone to make a picture of you with the hopes that it looked like the pictures of the players you were trying to look and sound like. (Hey, look at the picture on pages 48–49: That old boy in the middle either thinks or knows he's hot stuff and everybody has gathered around to commemorate that with a photo.) Sometimes, maybe for a few minutes, you might actually in your mind become one of them. Like on a Sunday afternoon on somebody's porch with a whole bunch getting right in straight-back armless chairs that you could really pick in and just picking until your fingers and your mind just swim with it. You could almost get to the point where there is nothing between your mind and the notes.

There's a lot of those feeling in these photos.

John Hartford

INTRODUCTION

SOUTHERN EXPOSURE gathers together photographs from the 1850s to the outbreak of the Second World War to capture a world of musical performers, black and white. Some are still known, others forgotten; some were famous in their day, others just ordinary "folk" making music for home and family. The pictures tell stories that the musicians themselves no longer can tell, and capture a time when music was an integral part of home, church, and work.

We chose this period because it is underrepresented in most books. The photos themselves often were saved by families as keepsakes, not created for reproduction. They were simply cherished as memories of earlier times and the people who lived in them. They have been "rediscovered" by folklorists and collectors sometimes as evidence of the musical practices of long ago, sometimes merely as conversation pieces or decorative mementos of a society that is gone.

An important source has been the Library of Congress's Farm Security Administration archives. In the 1930s, in an attempt to document the vanishing life of the southern farmer—and also to employ artists, photographers, anthropologists, and sociologists—the government embarked on a massive collecting campaign. These photos were taken by some of the greatest photographers of the time: Walker Evans, Russell Lee, Ben Shahn, Dorothea Lange, and many more. Thanks to the digitization of the full negatives from the FSA collections, many more images are becoming available on-line. And among the many activities pictured, not surprisingly music plays a major role.

The book is divided into sections. This occurred as relationships developed among the images—sometimes subjective ones—and the images themselves seemed to resonate with each other, so that one led naturally to another.

Our interest is in how the pictures tell stories—stories of the musical life of the southern states. These stories have to be understood in the broader context of two questions: What is southern music? And how is it popularly portrayed?

Who Are These Folk?

The debate over just what is folk music has raged for centuries. The folk-blues guitarist Big Bill Broonzy supposedly was asked for a definition of folk music. He was said to reply, "Well, I never heard no horse make music"!

Prior to the eighteenth century there was no division between "art" and "folk" music—because folk music as a whole was simply unrecognized. The only music worth noting was the art music played at church or court. And these two areas were closed off to the common person—the royal chapel was for the exclusive use of the nobility, and court events also catered to this highly privileged class.

With the growth of national identities and sense of indigenous culture, a few artists began to recognize the rich world of "folk music" that surrounded them. The music of the ordinary folk—farmers, miners, weavers, artisans, and craftspeople—was elevated to the status of a precious commodity, to be collected and studied. Folklorists set off on foot, horseback, or bicycle to collect the "original" music of the land—and published their collections in weighty tomes to fill academic and home libraries.

The founding of America corresponded with this blossoming interest in national culture. America itself was an assertion of a unique identity—something new under the sun, a gathering of diverse people to form a single, united country. Actually, most of the original Americans came from a small portion of Europe: Britain, France, and Spain. The British culture would dominate, just as the British Empire would end up governing most of colonial America. So it's natural that this initially would be the strongest influence on American music.

However, the nineteenth century brought many changes to the land. A small slave trade with Africa had been established in the late 1700s to supply much-needed laborers for America's farms. This grew into the mass forced migration of hundreds of thousands of people from central and western Africa, who brought a rich musical tradition with them. Although forbidden to make music in many places, they could not be stopped entirely from singing and playing music. And their close proximity to their white masters quickly led to an intermingling of musical cultures that would produce the richest strands of American music: blues, popular song, ragtime, and jazz.

Several other important migrations took place in the nineteenth century. The great Irish potato famine of the 1830s and 1840s would lead to thousands of people leaving their home country in search of better conditions in "Ameri-kay." The Irish would settle in several American cities—most notably Boston, New York, and Chicago—and develop rich musical cultures there. Germans and Welsh were brought to America because they had experience as coal miners in their homeland; the mining industry was booming here and desperately needed trained workers. After the Civil War, another flood of immigrants came—this time the first Eastern Europeans, Italians, and Swedes.

The various people who came willingly to the United States were attracted by the opportunity to start anew. For many, this meant becoming Americans—and leaving the old traditions behind. Thus came the image of America as the great melting pot, where many cultures were combined into one. But really these cultures were not lost in the new land—despite widespread predictions that there would be no more Italian, German, Irish, or African American music in America, the opposite seems to be true. Cultures have a way of preserving themselves despite the forces of assimilation.

And so American music might better be described as a musical stew than a smeltery, where different flavors combine and remix to be forever changing into new musical styles.

The Myth of the South

As powerful as the myth of the folk is the myth of the South. When we think of the southern United States, positive and negative images flood our minds: the aristocratic antebellum old South, with its southern belles and well-bred planters, versus the image of Ma and Pa Kettle, the rednecks and hillbillies who (supposedly) inhabit the southern backwoods. Cross-burning Klansmen and racial intolerance has been a sad part of the southern legacy; yet the flip side of this horrific image is the fact that blacks and whites have intermixed and mingled more strongly in the South than perhaps in any other region of the country.

There are similar myths about southern music. That southern musicians were illiterate, untrained, with no knowledge of "real" music. That only the lazy, untalented, or handicapped—who could find no other work—would entertain the idea of being a musician. That music was the "Devil's work," and not suitable for good, Christian folks. That folksingers sang—or played—"that way" because they couldn't sing—or play—"the right way."

Myths are powerful not only because they color the way we look at certain people—but because the people themselves can also adopt them. Much has been made recently of the imagery of country music. Garth Brooks dresses like a cowboy not because he was raised riding the range but because that is the acceptable garb for a country performer. Boots, hats, and spurs say "country" the way white tie and tails say "classical" or oversized jeans say "rap."

In a book of images, it's important to remember that imagery is something that is created, that from the first camera snap someone was thinking: *What picture am I trying to make? What story am I trying to tell?*

Family Gatherings

Many of the images here show people at home, enjoying music as a part of their daily activities. Today we are used to having portable cameras that, at a moment's notice, and in any light, can capture a "Kodak moment." But certainly in the nineteenth century and still to some extent in the early twentieth century, having a picture taken was an arduous process, and it was not as easy to take an informal shot as it is today. That these pictures were made is all the more remarkable.

Some are obviously posed, despite the attempt to give them an offhand air. The string band sitting outside of a fine southern home, instruments casually held, dressed in tuxedo-like suits, obviously knew they were being photographed. This kind of memorial photograph—whether for use in publicity or simply as a way of recording a specific gathering— helps us at least see some of the more famous bands as they might have appeared on stage, if not sitting around the home fireplace.

The memorial photograph of a family gathering was a time-honored image. We all like to gather the family around in front of the camera. The fact that in many of these images we see a banjo player among the relatives, or a fiddler and guitarist entertaining the assembled friends, is proof of how much music was a part of the common life.

One of my favorites of these images is the rural picnic shown on pages 22–23. Someone must have taken a bulky camera back into the fields to get this image, supposedly a relaxed one of people enjoying a day in the country, while making music on fiddle, guitars, and mandolin. But the musicians are dressed in finery that would have been easily spoiled if they were on a true walk through the fields, and the music making is obviously staged for the camera. But there's something entirely appropriate about the shot—it couldn't have existed if scenes like this one were total fabrications.

Truth or Publicity?

For many decades, the figure of blues guitarist Robert Johnson was a shadowy one. Where was he born? What did he look like? How did he live? These were questions difficult, if not impossible, to answer. Then, finally, two photographs of Johnson were found—two images that represent in miniature some of the ways that images shape and are shaped by our expectations. If either photo had been found without the other, our image of Johnson would be radically different. With both we are given two sides of a coin—and two choices from which to select our own, perhaps third, image.

One image, shown on page 144, is a photo-booth picture, rough and out of focus. In it a cigarette is drooping from Johnson's mouth. Part of the neck and body of a guitar is visible in his hands, but not so much that we can identify the instrument. Johnson is dressed casually, in worker's clothes, and goes hatless. He is staring at the camera grimly. The picture appears to have been taken on the run, as if Johnson were momentarily halted one day while he was practicing his music.

The other image, shown on page 147, is the diametric opposite. Johnson is dressed in a fine, three-piece, striped suit. He wears a fashionable hat, with the brim jauntily cocked on one side. He has an expensive striped silk tie around his neck, and a white shirt with a high collar. There is a handkerchief placed artfully in his breast pocket. He is wearing leather dress shoes. He holds his Gibson guitar in his hands, as if he were playing it—his right thumb has a pick on it, and the right index and third figure are picking up. His left hand is on the guitar neck, forming a chord. Johnson sits on a box that is draped with a fine patterned cloth. He is smiling broadly.

This photograph was taken by the Hooks Brothers Studio of Memphis—a leading portrait studio for African American patrons of the day. And Johnson would have paid top dollar to have this fancy portrait made. Today no blues musician would appear on stage dressed like this! But in those days blues performers did not dress in shabby worker's clothes—they were on the cutting edge of fashion, and as sharp as a knife. Pictures of both white and black country performers from the same period underscore this image—they are always dressed to the nines.

Which Johnson is the real man? Did he perform dressed in casual back-country clothes or dressed like a Nashville lawyer? Most blues singers—indeed most people, whether wealthy or poor—dressed up in their Sunday best when they sat for a photo portrait—if only because having their picture taken was such a rare and wonderful event.

Gus Cannon, a Memphis bluesman and banjo player who was featured in the influential Cannon's Jug Stompers, is also famously pictured in a formal dress suit—taken at the same Hooks Brothers Studio (see page 143). Could he have performed in such an outfit on Memphis's famous Beale Street? It certainly goes against our understanding of this being a rough-and-ready neighborhood. Perhaps the dress code for bars and brothels was more formal than we'd like to think.

But this begs the question of whether the picture shapes the image or captures it—and whether any collection of images (documentary or not) can be really an accurate depiction of what it supposedly portrays.

The Camera's Eye

When I first saw many of the pictures in this collection, I was astonished. I didn't expect to see family string bands sitting out on the back porch of their homes—men, women, and children nestling a wide variety of string instruments as comfortably as if they were born with them.

Some of these pictures are obviously portraits—like the formal picture of Robert Johnson—while others are just snapshots—like the photo-booth version of Johnson. The fact that a picture was created by a photographer doesn't make it less accurate. It simply adds to the mystery—one we can only understand by looking at all of the evidence.

Most of the rural string bands also posed in suit-and-tie, at least in publicity shots. Even in the nineteenth-century daguerreotypes that survive, we see stiffly standing fiddlers and banjo players sporting their Sunday finest, replete with bow ties carefully knotted and finely pressed suits. The famous publicity photo of Charlie Poole and His North Carolina Ramblers on page 133 shows a group that could be country lawyers—if they weren't holding musical instruments. Poole himself was described as a rough-living, heavy-drinking rounder, but here he is finely dressed with shiny shoes and black suit, not a hair out of place on his carefully combed head.

Some have argued that the suit-wearing musician was fighting the stereotype of the bibs-and-overalls that was the uniform of the backwoods rube. But, just as the three-minute limit on 78 rpm recordings artificially shortened many country performances, it's difficult to say how much the camera changed the image—or the image was purposely shaped for the camera.

Just ten years after Poole posed in his suit, typical string bands were putting forth another image. By the mid-1930s, rural acts were expected to look rural—*neat* rural, but rural nonetheless. Most band members wore cowboy clothing, including plaid shirts, the obligatory cowboy hats, and khaki trousers. But everything still looks artificially neat, like these cowboys spent more time at the cleaners than rustling on the range.

The Urge to Collect

In the late eighteenth century, a new idea swept through Europe: the importance of the "common people" and an appreciation for their art. Suddenly, folk songs and dance tunes were all the rage, and literary types with pencil and paper swept through Europe in search of this hidden art form.

The same wave eventually hit America, where a group of dedicated women and men began searching the South for folk songs and folkways. John Avery Lomax, one-time staff-member of the University of Texas and avid lover of cowboy songs, was one of the first and best-known. But there were many more: radical northern women like Mary Elizabeth Barnacle who befriended the famous singer/coal mining activist Aunt Molly Jackson and twelve-string blues guitarist Lead Belly; folklorist B. A. Botkin, who took a more academic and literary bent to his collecting; John W. Work III, one of the first African Americans to collect and treasure the music of his own people; and John Lomax's son Alan, who was the first great advocate for folk culture in our country.

For those interested in the visual history of folk performance, we are most fortunate that these pioneering collectors kept field notes (and many, like Alan Lomax, took photographs). Many of their "discoveries" were in turn photographed during the Depression years by a small army of government-employed photographers under the aegis of the federal Farm Security Administration (FSA) program. Some of these photographers went on to become among America's greatest photographic artists: Walker Evans established his career as one of our great documentary photographers in the Depression, finding poetry in everyday objects and scenes; Dorothea Lange went on to become one of America's most celebrated documentary photographers. Ben Shahn had a long and distinguished career as a painter and sculptor. And many of their images have become justly famous: Arthur Rothstein captured the heart of the Depression in his famous photograph of an Oklahoma farmer and his son fleeing to their home during a dust storm; Walker Evans's photos of farm families living in newspaper-lined shacks inspired a reform movement to bring electrification and water to the rural South.

In this book, we've tried to uncover some of the lesser-known images from the FSA and other collections. Many of these images have never been reproduced before. They have remained proudly in the hands of the descendants of the musicians who are portrayed in them. But whether anonymous or famous, they all give a picture of the musical culture of a time that can only be remembered, and only fleetingly relived.

Southern Exposure

This book examines many of these issues primarily through the pictures it presents. While providing some commentary on each image, we've tried to allow the images to speak for themselves. Whenever possible, the circumstances of how the image was created—or its original purpose, whether commercial or personal—is noted, for whatever insight that might offer.

These pictures capture a richness of musical culture and experience that is astonishing. Whatever the source of the music—passed from generation to generation or heard through the phonograph or radio—and whatever the source of the image—a natural or posed situation—the pictures speak eloquently of the richness of the southern musical experience. And, hopefully, they also speak eloquently to the deep roots of this music, which, despite the odds, is ever surviving and ever self-renewing.

THE LITTLE OLD LOG CABIN IN THE LANE

MUSIC MAKING AT HOME

ALL MUSIC MAKING begins at home, or so we like to think. Mothers and fathers pass their skills to sons and daughters, who in turn preserve the music of their childhood like so many pressed flowers and precious gems. But the image of what is home (and what is a family) has changed over the years, as can be seen in this group of photographs.

For many late-nineteenth-century white families, music making was a genteel entertainment, something to be enjoyed on a family outing such as a Sunday picnic, or as a parlor entertainment performed by the young women. Rowdier backwoods families—who would have felt that music making was inappropriate for women because of its association with hell-raising, including such immoral activities as drinking, fighting, and dancing—couldn't usually afford to have their photos taken, and therefore many fewer of these pictures have survived. So, in this chapter we see a more gentrified version of music making, as banjos and fiddles began to invade the front parlor of Victorian homes.

For the black families, music was often a second means of income—and thus more serious business. Musical capabilities could give a man a leg up in the community, allowing him to associate on a less formal basis with his white neighbors, and also to pull in much-needed dollars. But still, music was also something to be enjoyed when the day was done, and in images here we see black families both formally and informally making music, paralleling the musical culture of the white world.

The most striking contrast between the two cultures can be seen in the photos on pages 24–25 of Pete Steele and his family proudly standing on their porch in front of a tidy Victorian home juxtaposed with the black sharecropper playing his banjo in front of what appears to be a fairly typical, simple shack. The pride of the Steele family in their well-pressed clothing contrasts well with the black family in their more ragged, functional outfits; and the hard look on the black woman's face reflects the tougher world she faced as her husband cheerfully entertains the children with his banjo.

These two women dressed in their Sunday best are Agnes Thompson and Mattie Boner from Forsyth County, North Carolina. They have just come home from church, and are about to enjoy a Sunday afternoon singing. The guitar that Agnes is playing is a typical late-nineteenth-century parlor-type instrument. You can see from Agnes's picking hand that she's a fingerpicker—in other words, she picks the strings with her fingers, rather than strumming across them with a pick. This would have been the typical style of playing from the late nineteenth century through the 1920s. Her repertoire would probably have been the light classical and popular songs of the day. Judging from their hats, we imagine this photo is from the early '20s. Photo courtesy of Faye Fritts

Here is an early posed photo of a white rural string band. Note the harmonica player on the left end, the small-bodied guitar being played by the mustached fella in the hat, and the old-time style of holding the fiddle employed by the first fiddler from the left: He rests the instrument on his arm, pushing it against his chest. The next fiddler in line uses the more acceptable "classical" position. Note also the natty suits, vests, and Stetsons worn by the musicians—this was before either hillbilly or cowboy clothing was introduced as more acceptable for rural band members. It wasn't unusual to have a bowed cello or bass in the group; many bands, particularly from Mississippi, used a cello to provide the bass notes for the group. Notice the child's-size violin on the table with what appears to be a pile of harmonicas leaning on it. And, what's that fella doing on the left pointing a pistol at the fiddler? (Perhaps he's an opera fan. . . .) This photo probably dates from the 1880s. Photo courtesy of Jim Bollman

This image shows a black family string band photographed in Hammond, Louisiana, that in instrumentation is not that different from the white group seen on the previous pages. Again, there's a cello or bass, a small-bodied guitar, and a fiddle. Despite the fact that the home looks rather run-down, the musicians and their families are dressed in their Sunday clothes. Even the dog on the far left is well mannered, sitting up straight, in a formal pose. Like their white counterparts, they probably got their guitars through the mail-order catalogs of Sears, Roebuck or Montgomery Ward, which introduced inexpensive instruments into the South beginning at the turn of the century. Again, this photo dates from the late 1800s. Photo courtesy of the Corbis/Bettmann Archives

Here's a group of unknown North Carolina musicians photographed on an outing, probably around 1910–20. Of course, their fine clothes would have been totally inappropriate for a stroll in the fields—so it's clear that this was a preplanned photograph, not a snapshot. Nonetheless, it is a charming picture of what a family band might have looked like in the rural South around the turn of the century. Note that the fiddler holds the instrument against his upper chest, rather than under his chin. The two small-bodied guitars were typical of parlor instruments of the day; and the round-backed mandolin was also acceptable for a woman to play. The fiddle, being associated with rowdy dancing and high living, was not usually a woman's instrument. Note the hats and flowers carefully arranged at their feet. Photo courtesy of Bob Carlin

Here's a black family posed in front of what appears to be a sharecropper's shack—in contrast to the Steele family depicted in front of their white-painted home with its Victorian-like porch decoration (shown on the facing page). This image is almost a stereotype; the banjo player wears the kind of straw hat that a field hand would typically wear to keep his eyes out of the sun. Still, the wife's straightforward gaze and obvious pride in her appearance shows the strength of these people in the face of what must have been grueling poverty. And the banjoist is clearly absorbed in his music while his children play. Judging by his hand position, he's using the tradition-al "frailing" or "clawhammer" techniques. Although the actual date of the photo is unknown, we imagine it was taken in the late 1800s. Photo courtesy of Jim Bollman

Banjo player Pete Steele (center) poses with his family on the porch of their home, in a photograph probably taken in the late '20s or early '30s. Steele was a part-time banjo player and full-time coal miner who lived in southern Ohio. He is famous as the source of two songs, the banjo instrumental "Coal Creek March" and the protest song "Pay Day [at Coal Creek]." Both songs commemorated the hard times experienced by coal miners; the "Coal Creek March" was said to have been played to accompany a group of striking miners on parade. Steele was recorded in the late '30s by folklorist Alan Lomax for the Library of Congress's Archive of Folk Song, and again in the late '50s by Ed Kahn for a Folkways album. He played banjo in a two-fingered, up-picking style. Photo reproduced from the Collections of the Library of Congress

An unknown family poses in their living room for a formal portrait, probably taken around 1900. Although they hold musical instruments, there's something suspicious about this picture: The lady in the front row is "playing" a banjo that doesn't appear to have any tuning pegs or strings, while to her right another lady is "playing" a fan. Whether added for color or not, the banjo is a typical late-nineteenth-century instrument. The frets end well above the head, so the frailing-style banjo player could play the strings over the top of the neck rather than the head. The young woman in this picture has her picking hand held in a style more typical of parlor guitar than banjo. Photo courtesy of Bob Carlin

Not quite as genteel a family as those in the photograph on the previous page, here's a small family group with unusual instrumentation: a two-row button accordion (sometimes called a melodeon) accompanying a five-string banjo. Their dress is the typical work clothing of a farm family; they've made no attempt to "doll themselves up" for the camera. The accordion is a typical inexpensive model that could have been ordered through the mail, as is the banjo. Note the metal piece covering the fret board toward the head of the banjo; this allowed for playing over the neck. Also note the banjo player appears to be using a two- or three-finger plucking style, rather than frailing. Grandma doesn't look too happy with the music! This photo comes from around 1910.
Photo courtesy of Jim Bollman

Mattie and Essie Nance are two sisters, enjoying some fiddle and guitar music outside of their North Carolina home. Again, note the fine clothing that they're wearing. The guitar is slightly larger than the parlor instruments of the late nineteenth century, placing this photo probably in the '20s. Note that Essie holds the fiddle in the classical manner. Could they be playing dance tunes? Sentimental songs? Hymns? The photograph is silent; it's impossible to know. The fact that all types of music could be played by these two simple instruments shows the richness of the musical tradition. The fact that we assume that they're playing "Soldier's Joy" rather than "Nearer My God to Thee" says as much about us—as viewers—as it does about them as musicians. Photo courtesy of Glee Arnold

ROLL ON, BUDDY

RURAL AND INDUSTRIAL WORKING MUSIC

MUSIC MAKING is not limited to the home. For centuries, music has been used as a means of allaying the monotony of hard work. It is also a powerful means of coordinating a large group, so that hammers fall at the same time, or oars pull through the water smoothly. And music also has a way of bonding a workforce, creating a communal spirit, whether it be a small group of loggers or a large regiment of soldiers.

The images collected here span many different types of activities. The first show the cruel conditions under which blacks labored in the notorious prison farms and chain gangs of the South—probably not too different from the typical work gang that you might have seen on a pre–Civil War southern plantation. Indeed, the servitude of the African Americans did not end with the war. Many went directly from slavery to sharecropping—and had just about the same chance of escaping the hard life of farming as they did the shackles of slavery. And black prisoners were mistreated in ways that boggle the mind.

Yet, despite this tough existence, music flourished: gospel hymns that lifted the spirits; work songs that helped pass the time and coordinate the group effort; blues that expressed the despair at the tough conditions; and lighthearted dance music that was purely for entertainment.

A lucky few escaped this existence. A son of a sharecropper, named McKinley Morganfield, is pictured on pages 40–41 playing the guitar on the porch of his home, a plain rural shack. He would escape to Chicago where he took quickly to the life of a musician—trading his acoustic guitar for an electrified instrument, and his country name for the more evocative Muddy Waters.

Music making infiltrated all parts of southern life—from the cotton mills to the logging camps, from coal mines to group activities like barn raisings. In a second group of photos here, mostly candid shots taken by unknown hands, we can see how music filled the work life of the rural communities. A few of these photos may have been posed; well-heeled urban folks in the Victorian era liked putting photos of everyday life on their walls as a sign of their appreciation for the "simple folk" employed in the work of churning butter or shucking corn. But, posed or not, these photos give vivid testimony to the role of music in the old South, from one great war (the Civil War) to another (World War II).

This is an early photo of a black prison gang hoeing cotton, taken at the notorious Parchman Farm Prison in Mississippi, probably from the late 1800s. Because of its location in the Delta, and the fact that it was used as a jail for black criminals no matter how minimal their crimes, Parchman became the famous home to many blues performers—and the subject of many blues songs. To break the monotony of hard work, the gangs would often sing songs. These songs helped set the rhythm for the work and coordinate the working of the large group. Note the white overseer toward the middle of the row, dressed in the boater hat. Photo courtesy of Joe Vinikow

A group of black prisoners working with axes at Darrington State Prison Farm, Sandy Point, Texas. The leader of this small crew had the nickname of "Lightning." The group can plainly be seen singing in time to the movement of their axes. It appears that they are either breaking up hard ground or small stones. Chain gangs were among the cruelest—and most common—forms of punishment in the rural South. Even as late as the 1950s, gangs could be seen working on roads in their distinctive prison uniforms. The fact that gang members were able to transform this punishment into occasions for music making—and the richness of the music that was made—speaks to the importance of music not only as a means of regulating work but also of building hope. The photograph was taken in April of 1934.
Photo reproduced from the Collections of the Library of Congress

Another black prison gang, this time working with shovels, apparently pounding down the surface of a dirt road. Rhythmic work that required group coordination—whether it be lifting the heavy sails on a frigate, cutting through the hard rock of a coal mine, or settling the ground in order to lay a road—could best be coordinated by a call-and-response song. Work songs have been used for centuries; probably the slaves sang as they built the Egyptian pyramids. It is unknown who is the central figure, watching the scene; he could be a gang overseer or perhaps a visitor. This photograph was possibly taken at Cumins State Prison Farm in Gould, Arkansas, in 1934. Photo reproduced from the Collections of the Library of Congress

A railroad work gang lays track in Lufkin, Texas. The photo was taken by the well-known FSA photographer Russell Lee and may have been posed. Nonetheless, these workers appear to be dressed in typical clothing and performing the arduous labor of setting the ties individually. It's hard to imagine that the thousands of miles of railroad track were all "handmade"; but in fact it took much heavy labor, much of it performed by low-paid workers (many of whom were new immigrants to the United States), to lay the lines that linked the coasts. Like many other FSA photographers, Lee was trying to make a point in his photographs; he hoped that city dwellers would get a better idea of the rough conditions under which the less-fortunate workers struggled. In this way, he was documenting a scene with a purpose; and while the purpose may have changed, the scene lives on. The photograph was taken in April of 1939. Photo reproduced from the Collections of the Library of Congress

Henry "Son" Sims and McKinley Morganfield—aka Muddy Waters— photographed on the porch of Muddy's shack on Stovall's Plantation located in Clarksdale, Mississippi, the heart of the Delta country, taken in 1941. Before moving north to Chicago, Muddy was raised on a Mississippi plantation, plowing, hoeing, and cutting cotton from the age of ten. While searching for the legendary blues guitarist Robert Johnson in the summer of 1941, folklorist Alan Lomax came to Stovall and recorded and photographed Muddy and Son. Sims was a friend of legendary blues guitarist Charlie Patton, and recorded with him in 1929. Note that Muddy is holding a resonaphonic guitar (sometimes called a Dobro); it has a round metal plate set in the wooden body to give it extra volume. Two years later, Muddy left for Chicago and started a new life. Photo courtesy of the John W. Work III Field Collection, Center for Popular Music, Middle Tennessee State University

These two photographs show a typical rural workers' string band, probably photographed in the late 1800s. In the first photograph, a close-up, we can see how the fiddler on the left holds the instrument against his breast, while the one on the right takes the more traditional classical position. The guitarist is playing a typical small-bodied "parlor-type" instrument of the late nineteenth century with a classical-style head. His hand position also seems to indicate that he was picking the strings, rather than strumming them as is more common today as an accompaniment to dance music. He also appears to have been a smoker; note the cigarette that is lightly balanced on his outstretched shoe. In a second image, what appears to be the same band—perhaps photographed at the same time—is playing for a large group of appreciative farmhands. The workers are huddled around a large beer barrel. Note the man dressed in the bowler hat and suit coat—perhaps the farm's owner—who is posed holding the barrel's pump handle, while a second man to his right holds up a large glass of beer. Why the men were dressed up in coats and ties is unknown to us; perhaps this was a harvest celebration of some kind. Undoubtedly, it was a special event to have both music making and good drinks on hand. The fact that this was a spontaneous shot is underlined by the figures that are moving slightly whose faces are blurred. The fact that both photos may have been taken on the same day—and both survived—is quite unusual, attesting perhaps to the fame of the band itself or the wealth of the farm owner. Photos courtesy of Jim Bollman

The official band of the Cannon cotton mills of Kannapolis, North Carolina, known as the W.O.W. (Woodmen of the World) String Band. This group broadcast over local radio station WBT out of Charlotte. Many mills and mines sponsored bands as a means of building workers' morale. Sometimes they even subsidized uniforms, sent the bands out on the road (to promote their products, naturally), and sponsored radio shows. In the W.O.W. band, note the formal dress, the cello, and the rather high-quality instruments; two of the guitars appear to be arch-top jazz models, the latest thing at the time, circa 1935. Left to right are: Carl Dayvault (guitar), Raymond Thornburg (cello), Shell Allen (fiddle), Haywood Suther (banjo mandolin), and Adolphus Dayvault (guitar). Photo courtesy of Rachel Wiles

A small farm group peel and prepare the apples to make apple butter, while a banjo player entertains them. This has the look of a semiposed picture, but nonetheless it has enough authenticity about it to ring true to life. This photo was from the 1880s, taken at a time when images of folk activities were increasingly popular in urban homes. City dwellers could get a taste of the "quaint" folk practices of the countryside without leaving their homes by hanging these photos on their walls. Pictures like these were kind of photographic versions of Colonial Williamsburg, if you will. Photo courtesy of the Corbis/Hulton-Deutsch Collection

Logging camp workers take a break to pose for a group picture. And sure enough one of them has a banjo! This rough and wild crowd includes two women (at back) who probably served as cooks. Thanks to mail-order catalogs that spread inexpensive instruments from coast to coast, thousands of musicians could afford good-quality guitars, banjos, and mandolins—where previously they may have struggled to make homemade replicas. While not exactly cream-of-the-crop instruments, they served the purpose of bringing a reasonable level of quality to amateurs and would-be performers. And, for those working in logging camps or mines, the banjo was an ideal, portable means of amusement. This photo dates from the 1920s. Photo courtesy of Jim Bollman

These World War I soldiers hailed from rural North Carolina and brought their music with them to France, where this photo was taken. Again, it is a posed picture, to show off the fancy guns and the banjo. Left to right are: Lee Hillingin, Cyrus Lineberry, Jacob Harvell, and Marcus Johnson. Lee is holding Jake's banjo, further proof that this shot was posed. The three men on the right are all from Cedar Falls, North Carolina, and the photo was taken in the teens. Banjo-playing youth were among the many people swept from the countryside to participate in World War I. It's not surprising they would take a small piece of their home culture—like a banjo—with them, to display proudly and to remind them of their home lives. Photo courtesy of the Harvell family

Cotton mills and coal mines were the two major employers in the South. And many of these companies sponsored string bands as a way of keeping the workers entertained. This band was the official group of North Carolina's Spray Mill Company, photographed circa 1900. They are arranged hierarchically in rows of fiddlers, guitarists, and banjo players, with the then-common bowed double bassist standing to one side. We know the names of these musicians, which is unusual for a photo from this period. In the first row, left to right, are: Blat Hailey, Sam Hutson, and John Kallam; the second row: John Hackney, Lee Wade, Bud Forbs, John Land, and Will Barker; and the third row has Haymon Newman, Percil Hailey, Jim Barksdale, and Bob Martin. Photo courtesy of Kinney Rorrer

Just as in World War I, soldiers in World War II brought country music to the front. This photo was taken in 1944 in Leicester, England. It shows guitarist Frederic Anderson playing with Snowden Risner on the fiddle. Note the large-bodied, F-holed jazz-style guitar that Anderson plays. By this time, jazz influences were strongly felt in country music—not only in the type of instruments, but also in the more "swinging" feel given to the music itself, and in its repertoire, which included many more popular songs. The photo is silent as to the type of music being played—but we can imagine that it had a certain lilt to it that spoke to the jazz era, even if it hearkened back to the music of home. Photo courtesy of Snowden Risner

Rosin the Bow

FOLK INSTRUMENTS AND THEIR PLAYERS

THREE INSTRUMENTS are associated most strongly in our minds with southern music: fiddle, banjo, and guitar. And indeed these are the most prevalent in the culture.

The fiddle is probably the oldest, coming with the original British, Scotch, and Irish settlers. They brought with them a rich tradition of dance music, which became the backbone of the American social dance repertoire—tunes like "Soldier's Joy," which (under the name "The King's Head") had folks tapping their feet in seventeenth-century England.

The banjo is one of those unique American mixtures, a product of the unintentional mixing of African and American cultures. Based on a skin-headed string instrument from Africa, the banjo itself has many features of the European guitar. And its music is also a mix of black and white, so deeply entangled that no one thread can be cleanly traced.

The guitar was first introduced in America as a parlor instrument for young ladies, enjoying a vogue after the Civil War as an ideal instrument for accompanying sentimental songs. It quickly spread—thanks largely to mail-order companies and the growth of small music stores—and found a place in all levels of society. More portable than a piano, more flexible than a banjo, the guitar soon became the number one instrument to accompany the voice—a role it has maintained to this day.

The unsung hero in the spread of unusual musical instruments throughout the South has got to be Rural Free Delivery, an innovation of the U.S. Postal Service that made mail-order businesses suddenly possible—and immensely profitable. Sears, Roebuck and Montgomery Ward brought lavishly illustrated catalogs to the hands of even the poorest farmer—where he could purchase inexpensive guitars, banjos, and fiddles, but also more exotic instruments like autoharps, mandolins, and small accordions. Because many of the happy buyers didn't know how to play these instruments, they had to come up with their own methods—sometimes successfully and other times not—which, in turn, created entirely new styles of music.

Of course, immigrant cultures also had a hand in spreading these instruments. German settlers in the Southwest brought their wide variety of accordions with them, and the loud instrument was soon a dance hall favorite—it could be heard much better over the din of stamping feet than the older fiddle. Traveling teachers would sell instruments on the age-old time plan ("A dollar down, and a dollar a week . . ."), thus encouraging musical literacy.

And then there are instruments—like the hammer dulcimer, an ancient instrument that dates back to biblical times—that crop up in certain parts of the country for reasons no one can know. Why is there a rich tradition of dulcimer playing in Michigan and West Virginia but not elsewhere? Perhaps a single talented individual settled in one place, inspiring a group of others to learn the instrument. Or perhaps an old instrument was abandoned, only to be rediscovered by newer players. No one can tell for sure.

The banjo was first popularized in the 1840s and 1850s through traveling circus and minstrel performers. The banjo has been traced to various African stringed instruments that featured animal-skin-covered sound boxes. For years, early minstrel performer Joel Walker Sweeney was given the credit for "inventing" the five-string banjo; this is undoubtedly untrue, although he may have contributed to its modern design. Early minstrel banjos may have four, five, eight, or more strings. Because instruments were essentially handmade, they could be custom built to almost any specification. It wasn't until the 1870s and 1880s that builders began mass-producing instruments—or at least making them in larger quantities—which led to a single design. This photo shows an unknown banjo player photographed around 1890 in Hope, Arkansas. Although dressed in his Sunday finery, including a gold watch fob, he's still a tough-looking fellow. Note that the photo is a reverse (backward) print; this is typical of early photographic prints. The fifth string peg appears to be on the wrong side of the banjo's neck, for this reason. Photo courtesy of Bob Carlin

Two images taken by FSA photographer Ben Shahn in Asheville, North Carolina, in 1937. The fiddler is Bill Henseley; in the second image, he is accompanied by Jeeter Gentry on banjo and Ernest Thompson on guitar and harmonica. The group was gathered to compete at the Asheville Folk Festival. This is a fairly typical lineup for an informal rural string band. Note that Henseley holds the fiddle low, against his collarbone, rather than under the chin. He also angles it more deeply toward the bow. Notice also the harmonica holder worn around the neck by Thompson; a nice innovation, this enabled the musician to handle two instruments at once. Gentry appears to be playing the banjo in the two-finger, up-picking style common among North Carolina musicians. All are dressed in suits, although they appear a little ragged on the edges. Photos reproduced from the Collections of the Library of Congress

A rural fiddler, Mrs. Mary McLean, at her home in Skyline Farms, Alabama, photographed by Ben Shahn in 1937. Notice the unusual way that she holds the fiddle—balanced against the lower shoulder blade, angled toward the bow, a typical southern traditional way of holding the instrument. She is deeply intent on her music making—a second, more famous image, shows her grinning broadly. The rooster in the barnyard seems to be enjoying the show. Photo reproduced from the Collections of the Library of Congress

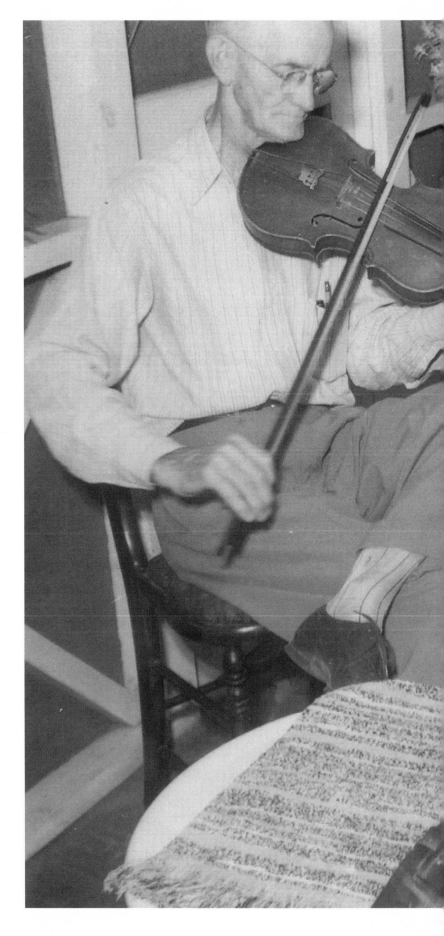

A rural string band from Ramseur, North Carolina, featuring fiddler Vaughn Marley, Glenn Davis on banjo, and hammer dulcimer player Tom Cox. The hammer dulcimer is another instrument with a long history—it dates back at least to the medieval era, and is found in Persia, Eastern Europe, and patches of Scotland and Ireland. The instrument is not related to the three-string Appalachian dulcimer; and neither is related to the "dulcimer" mentioned in the Bible. The hammer dulcimer is a kind of "piano without the middle man." The player holds two small wooden "hammers" in his or her hands, and strikes the strings directly. The strings are arranged so that they cross a bridge, dividing the strings into a 3:2 ratio, creating a perfect fifth. That is to say that if a "C" sounds on one side of the bridge, then a "G" will sound on the other. The dulcimer came to this country with Scottish, Irish, and German immigrants, and has settled in pockets of the South, as well as Michigan. The photo is from the 1940s. Photo courtesy of Vaughn Dorsett

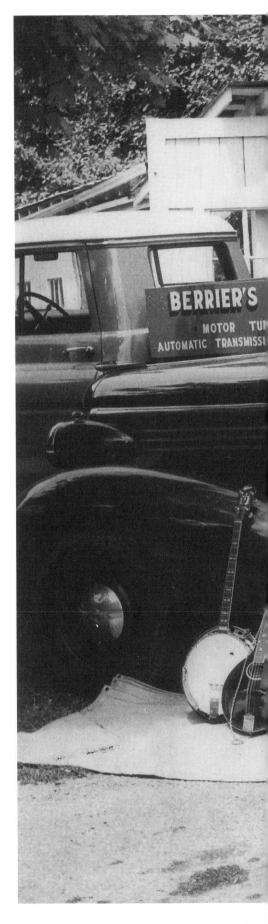

Olin Berrier poses in front of his garage in Welcome, North Carolina, circa 1950. This was a "set-up" photograph by a newspaperman, playing on the fact that Berrier was a mechanic by day and fiddler by night. This auto repairman and part-time musician took both his job and his hobby seriously. Notice he's playing the fiddle with a screwdriver instead of a bow! From left to right you see a tenor banjo; a Gibson A-style mandolin; a long-neck tenor; a ukulele; a Gibson flat-top guitar; another A-style mandolin lying on its side; a Gibson F-holed, arch-top guitar; a violin; a Gibson mastertone five-string banjo; another fiddle lying on its side; another five-string banjo; Berrier holding his fiddle; and a bass! Berrier worked hard to be able to afford this lavish assortment of instruments, which would have been expensive (relatively speaking) even in their day. Photo courtesy of Donna Michael

This famous photograph of two zydeco musicians was taken by FSA photographer Russell Lee in New Iberia, Louisiana, circa 1935. It has been often reproduced, for good reason. The photograph was taken on the day of the National Rice Festival, in Crowley, Louisiana, and the musicians were obviously well dressed in anticipation of entertaining the crowd. They haven't yet straightened and tightened their ties—it was a hot day, and they probably were posing before their performance. The accordion player holds a typical single-row button accordion. He is accompanied by another musician on washboard. The accordion came to this country in various forms with German, Eastern European, and Irish immigrants. First invented in the 1830s, the instrument went through several stages of development before the well-known piano-keyboard version evolved. It was also sold under different names—bandoneon, melodeon, concertina. . . . Button accordions or melodeons are the most common in Cajun music—and most are simple, single-row instruments like this one. Photo reproduced from the Collections of the Library of Congress

White Cajuns also played the accordion. Here's the famous husband and wife duo of Cleoma and Joe Falcon. They are recognized as the first Cajun artists to release a 78 rpm record, Allons à Lafayette, in 1928. Cleoma also came from a musical family, and recorded separately with her brothers, Amidie and Ophy Breaux, that same year. Cleoma holds a fairly ornate small-bodied guitar, probably made in the late nineteenth century. This would have been a fairly expensive instrument at the time. Joe is playing a typical single-row melodeon. This instrument featured a single row of buttons, playing in one key, and had four stops—the stops would enable you to access additional banks of reeds to double the melody in octaves. It only had two chord buttons. Photo courtesy of Bluebird Press, Eunice, Louisiana

Here's another group of musicians performing at the
National Rice Festival, again photographed by Russell
Lee in 1935. Hawaiian music was tremendously popular
in the South, beginning in the late nineteenth century
with touring groups of "authentic" Hawaiian players.
This Cajun native is playing a lap steel guitar in the
Hawaiian style. The guitar is a flat-bodied, electric
instrument. It is held on the lap, tuned to an "open tuning" (so, if you brush across the strings, you play a chord),
and barred with a steel or glass rod. Notice that he is
accompanied by a player (whose head has been cut off in
the photo) of a National Steel Guitar. These steel-bodied
instruments were popular among street musicians in the
days before electric amplification was common. Because
they had steel bodies—with a built-in resonator chamber
in the instrument's belly—they were very loud and
metallic sounding, perfect for blues or slide work. Two
Boy Scouts are seen behind the musicians, enjoying the
show. Photo reproduced from the Collections of the
Library of Congress

Nothing shows the fad for Hawaiian instruments better than this be-leied group of southern musicians, McKinley McDaniel's Hawaiian Concert, photographed sometime in the 1920s. Both musicians in the front row are holding standard guitars on their laps; again these would have been tuned to "open tuning" and barred with a steel or glass slide. In the back, notice on the left the banjo ukulele (a uke with a banjo body), guitar, and what is probably a tenor uke. All the musicians wear white natty clothes and matching shoes—this is one hot outfit! They don't look very pleased to be photographed, however. The stern looks may have come from holding the pose for a while for the camera. Photo courtesy of Agnes Thompson

Unknown North Carolina couple with an autoharp, photographed circa 1890. The auto-
harp was a late-nineteenth-century invention designed to help bring "music to the masses"
in the days before the phonograph. Its inventor, C. F. Zimmerman, had invented a new—
and what he believed to be simpler—method of music notation that would enable even
"unskilled" musicians to play popular songs. He invented the autoharp as a teaching aid for
his notation system. It spread quickly through the South thanks to mail-order catalogs from
Sears, Roebuck and Montgomery Ward—the same catalogs that brought inexpensive guitars,
banjos, and mandolins there. While some would simply push down the chord bars and
strum against the strings, others developed a more intricate method of playing melodies.
They would hold the autoharp up against their chests, and pick the strings using metal
guitar picks. Among the most famous autoharp players were the Carter family and Ernest
Stoneman, both of whom recorded in the '20s and '30s, and Kilby Snow, a virtuoso player
who was "discovered" in the late '50s. Photo courtesy of Bob Carlin

Heavenly Light Shine on Me

MUSIC AS PART OF WORSHIP AND CEREMONY

RELIGION AND RITUAL are key parts of southern life—and not surprisingly music has invaded these areas as well. Whether it be a traditional religious ceremony, a loose adaptation of a church practice, or an ancient practice drawn from centuries-old folk rituals, music is there.

The church has long taken a mixed view of music. On one hand, the musician is seen as an evil person; he or she lives outside of the social norms, and doesn't "work" for a living. The musicians' work includes accompanying dancing; dancing, in the church's view, inspires mixing of the sexes (outside of marriage!). Rural dances often were accompanied by heavy drinking, which in turn led to brawls and even murders. So, music was a powerful force for evil, in the church's mind.

On the other hand, music could lift the soul. A great hymn could inspire the parishioner to a better understanding of the Bible's message. Music was a great unifier, holding a congregation together. And music was a natural part of ritual—without it the procession would be sterile and dry.

Luckily for southern musicians, the Baptist Church was more open to music making than the Catholic Church. Many churches became centers for all-day hymn singing, and the parishioners were taught to read musical scores through the shape-note method. Shape notes were invented in the eighteenth century as a means of teaching nonmusic readers how to read music; different shapes—such as diamonds, squares, or circles—would represent different scale tones. Placed on the musical staff, the shape of the melody could be quickly seen in its rising and falling, so that many could learn their parts without being able to read traditional music notation.

But this group of photos doesn't only show traditional church procedures. You'll see here some pretty unusual rituals—ranging from southern Louisiana's Cajun Mardi Gras to one of the strangest rituals of the old South, the "womanless wedding." In many ways, these holdovers from traditional folk ceremonies were as important—if not more so—than the formal rituals of the church.

*A revivalist family group singing in a town square on a Saturday afternoon, in
Tahlequah, Oklahoma, photographed by Russell Lee in July of 1939. This appears to
be a family group, gathered around a guitarist, and preaching through their music
to a small crowd that has gathered to hear them perform. The guitar has a pie-plate-
type resonator in its body. Roving bands of revivalists were common in the South
and West, and often used music as a means of attracting the crowd—and to express
their deep-felt faith. Breaking up the musical performances with street preaching,
the evangelists hoped to spread the "message of the gospel" directly to the people.*
Photo reproduced from the Collections of the Library of Congress

The group has now become inspired, as they are joined by a drummer, and appear in ecstatic concentration. Through music, the performers could literally be filled with the Holy Spirit—like congregants who suddenly begin speaking in tongues or ecstatically dancing. The music-making experience takes them to a higher ground. This is a common experience, even among dance hall musicians who feel the uplift and joy of music making without equating it with any religious meaning. Here, obviously, the music has taken over, and the singers momentarily forget their listeners in the rapture of the moment. Behind the drummer, a woman is playing what appears to be a mandolin, with an odd, pear-shaped body. This may be a National metal-bodied instrument. Photo reproduced from the Collections of the Library of Congress

As gospel music became popular, family groups of semiprofessional musicians would take to the radio to spread the word. This unidentified group has a typically eclectic array of instruments: vibraphone, bass, trumpet, saxophone, accordion, piano, and, in the hands of the small child, a banjo ukulele. The preacher/leader sits at the microphone holding his Bible. The purpose of these groups was not to amuse their audiences—hence the serious expressions—but rather to inform. To get them on their feet, for sure, but in praise of the Lord. Photo courtesy of Bob Carlin

The Gospel Hour

Many ceremonial occasions beyond the church were occasions for music making. This large family is gathering in celebration of a birthday—perhaps of the man in the center in the suit and hat? Off to the right are the entertainers, a group of fiddlers and a banjo player. Everyone is dressed in their finery, with the women in white gowns. Life events— births, deaths, weddings, even the changing of the seasons—have long been "excuses" for music making. In many cultures, the music is an integral part of the event; for it to properly be completed, music must *be made. Which raises the age-old question: Which came first—the celebration or the song?*
Photo courtesy of Bette Sowers

Another important ceremony was the "school exhibition" or graduation. Just as today, schools liked to take a moment—usually at the term's end—to celebrate the completion of the year. It was a moment for adults to take pride in the achievement of their children, and for children to show off their newfound knowledge. And, of course, music was a part of the celebration, if only to add another level of grandeur to the festivities. This school exhibition occurred in the '20s at Whiteheart School, located in Davidson County, North Carolina. On the wagon is a celebratory band of adults, come to entertain the somewhat unruly gathering of school-age graduates. Photo courtesy of the Darr family

Here's a truly unique rural ceremony: a "woman-less" wedding! According to folklorist Jane Woodside, this is a parody of the Protestant wedding ceremony. Found in both black and white traditions—although more commonly among whites—womanless weddings were used as fundraisers as well as for their entertainment value. Begun in the early twentieth century, they became so popular that—beginning in 1918—"scripts" were published so that any group could put on its own womanless wedding. Many of these scripts were based on nineteenth-century "country" dramas. Notice the little "baby" at the front of the gathering. The musicians in the photo, left to right, are: Dewey, Bob, and Clay Everhart (on guitars and banjo) and Charlie Knight (in the dress, on fiddle). This picture dates from the mid-1940s. Photo courtesy of Ruth Everhart Coffey

Mardi Gras is an important celebration, and not just in New Orleans. Here's a costumed fiddler preparing for the Cajun Mardi Gras celebration, with his mask poised over his head. The fiddler is Wade Frugé. Rural Mardi Gras celebrations are less formalized than the tourist-attraction parades of the cities. Music making and dancing—whether formally in an old barn or community hall, or informally on a street corner—are all-important parts of the celebration. Roving, masked musicians—participating in holiday festivities marking the changing of the seasons—have been seen in many cultures for centuries. This Cajun update of an age-old figure is just one of the latest manifestations. This photo is from the mid-1940s.
Photo courtesy of Ann Savoy

This photo combines illusion and reality in some interesting ways. Taken circa 1925, it shows members of an eastern band of the Cherokee nation. However, they are not dressed in their traditional Native American clothing—which would probably not have been easily identified by the average viewer. Instead they are decked out in stereotypical "Indian" clothes. What we have here are Indians dressed as Indians! It was not unusual for performing Indians to adopt generic Indian-type clothing that would quickly identify them to the audience—just as country performers took to wearing stylized cowboy garb. The photo shows the brothers Ernest (guitar) and Osey Helton (fiddle) in Indian-style headdress, and their niece Costine. Photo courtesy of Charity Gates

DANCE ALL NIGHT, DANCE A LITTLE LONGER

MUSIC FOR DANCING AND RECREATION

WHAT WOULD MUSIC BE without dancing? In the South, the traditional folk dances performed in both "big circles" and "squares" were an important part of everyday communal life and celebrations. And where there was dancing, there was music.

An English music publisher named John Playford published a small book in 1651 called *The Compleat Dancing Master* that set off a revolution. The book would go through many editions in Playford's lifetime—and was maintained in newer editions into the next century by his heirs. The book captured the music for folk and traditional dances performed in two parallel lines (known as country or contra dances) as well as dances performed by couples in a ring. Long beloved in the English countryside, these dances now were available to an urban audience—perhaps representing the first "folk revival"!

It is not surprising that these dances made their way to the United States. In the northeastern part of the country, the contra dance has been the strongest survivor. Here couples face each other in two parallel lines—like in the "Virginia Reel"—performing figures that move them up and down the sets.

In different parts of the South, big-circle or square dances were more popular. In the big-circle dance, couples alternately perform figures together and then, opening out into a full circle, the entire group will perform a figure—such as the "grand right and left," where the men progress around the circle in one direction while the women move in the other.

The "square dance" as we know it today is the product of many hands. Dance collectors went south and began notating steps. These steps were simplified and codified, and put into books. In the late nineteenth and early twentieth century, the physical fitness movement—along with a renewed interest in folk cultures—led to the teaching of square dancing to young children, often along with other European "ethnic" dances.

In the 1930s, with the new interest in cowboy life, Western square dancing was popularized. Here, a regular pattern of steps was taught. Dancers could "progress" from level to level, earning badges of recognition along the way. Western-square-dance groups across the country would all perform the same dances in the same way—making it possible to hold competitions among groups.

But the photos in these pages show a simpler, more natural square and big-circle dance style. Everything from the virtuoso solo dancing of clogging to the group big-circle dance is shown as it occurred in a time before it was necessary to be taught how to dance. Dancing was something that naturally occurred, and anyone—flat-footed or not—could participate.

A charming photograph of fiddler James Scotten playing for his niece as she step dances on his front porch in Holly Springs, North Carolina. Their affection for each other is obvious—as is their love of music and dance. Dances could be performed with just one instrument and one dancer as well as in a big crowd. Front porches made ideal "platforms" for backwoods step dancers, because of their resonant, raised, wooden flooring. You just can't get the same percussive sound on hard dirt—and gravel would trip up your feet! This photo dates from the 1930s. Photo courtesy of Will Scotten

This series of images are from a square dance held at the Skyline Farms, Alabama, photographed by Ben Shahn in 1937. Shahn, a professional painter and one of the greatest of the Depression-era American artists, captures the informal "frolic" in all of its unplanned glory. In this big-circle dance the caller is in the center calling the figures, while all the dancers circle. Figures would be performed by couples and then the men and women would circle in counterclockwise rings to take new partners. Photo reproduced from the Collections of the Library of Congress

Couples swing after promenading around the circle. Big-circle dances used many of the same figures as the more familiar square dance—the promenade, do-si-do, birdy in the cage—but they were incorporated into the circular formation. Unlike the square dance, the big-circle dance did not have to have eight couples to make it work. You could accommodate "as many as will," in the words of many old English dance manuals. The camera freezes a rather chaotic moment in the progression of the dance. Photo reproduced from the Collections of the Library of Congress

The circle moves. This is perhaps the most dynamic moment in the big-circle dance. The individual couples have performed their figures. Now the group moves as a whole—in a sweeping pattern of skirts and boots. Such ring dances date back centuries, and probably have ritual roots. Whatever rituals accompanied dances like these in the past, here the dancers enjoy the pattern of the movements as an end in itself. Photo reproduced from the Collections of the Library of Congress

This three-person dance team performs at Cumberland
Homesteads in Crossville, Tennessee. This is more of a show
dance figure than the group participatory figures depicted
in the previous photos. Even at this early date, dancers
would compete for prizes by performing showy specialized
figures or steps. Rather than being an occasion for group
celebration, these dances were performed for the enjoyment
of the viewers—and for a possible prize for the dancers.
Photographed by Ben Shahn, circa 1937. Photo reproduced from the Collections of the Library of Congress

This is a most-unusual shot of an all-black group of musicians. They are either visiting a white-owned farm or are workers who were taking a break to entertain their white employers. Their clothing combines elements of finery—vests, topcoats—with tattered hard-used items, like battered hats. Notice the fiddler plays in the traditional style, holding the fiddle low and against his chest. The banjo player appears to be frailing. His inexpensive instrument is adorned with many bracelets around the head—a typical way of "dressing up" an instrument. At the far right of the image a well-dressed white listener enjoys the music, with his left foot jauntily crossed in front of his right leg—almost as if he were moved to dance to the music. This photo probably dates to the late nineteenth or early twentieth century. Photo courtesy of Jim Bollman

A small-town dance band playing for a set dance. Left to right are: Zack Whitaker on cello, E. R. Echerd, the caller, Mrs. Elizabeth Nelson (partially hidden) at the piano, Clyde Pegram on fiddle, and Obie Peoples on banjo. Many rural string bands featured cello players to provide the low bass notes to support the melody. In fact, with probably only a few musicians available, dancers and bands had to make do with whomever they could find; and so a wide variety of expected and unexpected instruments might turn up in a dance band. A dancer is seen at the right edge of the frame. Photo, taken in 1941, by Carol W. Martin. Photo courtesy of Frances Allred

A Lion's Club Square Dance held in Lexington, North Carolina, in December of 1947. This was probably a special Christmas dance, calling for a large and impressive band. Left to right are: Hubert Lohr, Shorty Cruise, Olin Berrier (the mechanic whom we first met on pages 64–65), Ernest Harrington, Raymond Russell, Tom Cooper, and caller Russell Smith. Just as today, square dancing was popular as a means of drawing people to meetings of local fraternal and charitable groups, or of raising money for their efforts. The use of a microphone for the caller and several small speakers show how modern technology was beginning to creep into the dance scene. Note also that most of the musicians are dressed in Sunday suits; only one guitarist has opted for a cowboy shirt. Photo courtesy of Jeanne Beck

I Ain't Got No Home

STREET MUSICIANS AND SEMIPROFESSIONALS

THE MUSICIAN HAS ALWAYS BEEN a wanderer. Disenfranchised from the rest of society, he or she must travel from town to town, relying on the nickels and dimes of strangers.

For many rural musicians, music became a full-time career only due to a tragic circumstance, such as blindness or some other infirmity that did not allow them to "work" in a more ordinary job, such as farming or mining. Thus a musical career was not usually a choice, but a necessity—and the ability to move a crowd through either intensity of performance or virtuosity on the instrument became very important.

This was particularly true for black Americans. While white families could support their infirm members, blacks had barely enough to support themselves. So the blind and infirm had to make their way on their own. Myths grew up around the special musical powers that they had—as if to compensate for their lack of vision or mobility, God had given them special capabilities to bend a string or sing a song.

And, it is important to remember, for many black and white musicians there were few employment alternatives—beyond hard work in coal mines, farms, or cotton mills. For some, music became a second means of income. For others, who were attracted by the lure of the road, the freedom from responsibility, and the economic opportunity opened up by the growth of the recording, radio, and live performance industries, music was an ideal lifestyle.

As cities grew, a potential audience—with lots of loose change—was discovered by these street-corner musicians. They were not seeking to be famous recording stars (although some had had recording careers at one point or another) but merely trying to scrape enough together to buy food and drink. Even famous blues performers like Blind Willie McTell could end up begging on the streets. In the '50s the once-prolific recording star of the late '20s could be heard on Atlanta's streets playing his twelve-string guitar for pennies. America's musical memory is short—and the once-famous may quickly find themselves on the streets again, where much music making began.

Two images of a blind street fiddler and guitarist photographed on the streets in West Memphis, Arkansas, in October of 1935 by Ben Shahn. Some children listen. Note, unlike many rural fiddlers, this fiddler holds the instrument in a more-or-less traditional position. These musicians may be "Blind Pete" and George Ryan, a fiddle and guitar duo who were recorded in nearby Little Rock, Arkansas, on September 27, 1934, by folklorist John Avery Lomax. Often the field photographers would follow in the footsteps of collectors like Lomax, knowing that they could find musicians where he had previously worked. Both musicians are well dressed even though they are performing on the street. Photo reproduced from the Collections of the Library of Congress

A famous image of street musicians in Maynardville, Tennessee, photographed by Ben Shahn in October 1935. The image has widely become associated with the hard times of the Depression. This photograph is one of many that show Shahn's skills in making a "composition," undoubtedly influenced by his training as a painter. The image is powerful and speaks for itself; details like the fine suits, now tattered from hard use, tell us that these proud men were once well employed, but now have to make a living as best they can. Did their car break down and now, hoping to raise cash for its repairs, they're playing for passersby? Photo reproduced from the Collections of the Library of Congress

A blind African American man poses on the street with his children, one of whom holds a drum, another a triangle, while a third holds a tambourine. This street musician probably used his children as a means of gaining extra sympathy—and hopefully more cash. Across the top of his hat are the words "Help the Blind." He appears to be picking the banjo in a two-finger style. This photo comes from the late nineteenth century. He may have been singing on the street as a means of advertising a service or selling other goods; street singers hawking fruit or scrap metal were common in the South. Or, he may have been using his music to spread the gospel; religious street singers and preachers were also a common sight. Whatever his motivations, his daily take must have been small. While this photograph may have been posed, it certainly captures the rough life of the street musician hoping to raise a few pennies for his family. Photo courtesy of the Corbis Archives

Street musicians photographed near Scotts Run, West Virginia, in October 1935 by Ben Shahn. Again, even though he is a street musician, the guitarist wears a suit jacket and is seated with a well-dressed group of friends. Judging from his hand position, he probably is a fingerpicker. The guitar, with a slotted head, is a typical small-bodied flat-top model that could be purchased inexpensively from the 1860s through the 1920s and 1930s. While the musician is absorbed in his music making, with a slightly amused look on his face, the others stare suspiciously at the camera. Photo reproduced from the Collections of the Library of Congress

Street singer photographed near Skyline Farm, Alabama, by Ben Shahn, at the same time in 1937 that he photographed the square dancers, pictured on pages 92–95. A second musician, on the left, is partially blocked; he is playing a mandolin. Singers like this one would often perform spontaneously at events like dances, either to amuse themselves or to pick up some pocket change. Judging by his coveralls, this musician was probably a farmer or some kind of laborer, and pursued music making at most as a hobby. Photo reproduced from the Collections of the Library of Congress

By the '50s, it would have been rare to see music-makers on the street. In this case, Clay Everhart (banjo) and Larry Beam (guitar) were photographed on the streets of Lexington, North Carolina, simply because there was more light outside. The noise of modern cities—and the advent of transistor radios, Walkmans, boom boxes, and now cell phones—has pretty much put an end to the street-singing tradition. Yet, you still see guitarists in parks and on corners with their cases open—still strumming for loose change. Photo courtesy of Larry Beam and Ruth Everhart Coffey

Blind street singer Ernest Thompson was photographed May 7, 1943, on the streets of Winston-Salem, North Carolina. Some passing soldiers joined him in harmonizing. Published in the local newspaper, this image has a decidedly staged look. Nonetheless, this was a common scene on southern streets in the war years. Thompson is playing what appears to be a twelve-string, arch-top Gibson guitar. Notice the sign on Thompson's bowler, indicating that he is blind, and the collection cup he wears attached to his harmonica holder. For many blind people who could not work in fields or factories, music was the only means of support. Photo courtesy of David Hodges

DON'T GET WEARY, CHILDREN

RAGTAG CHILD BANDS

THIS SECTION HIGHLIGHTS the next generation of music-makers, the sons and daughters of musicians. As we have already stated, the family is the heart and soul of musical life. We hear our first lullabies from our mothers and fathers. We learn our first notes from our older siblings, sometimes in fierce competition to best them. Music thus is a birthright for those born to be the carriers of the tradition.

Of course, young people are also innovators. They hear the music of their fathers and mothers as hopelessly outdated. They want to be hip, cool, of the moment. And in the '20s and '30s, to be hip in the South was to catch the latest trends. These included Hawaiian-styled music and clothing, both of which were tremendously popular. So, suddenly, we see "young Hawaiians" sprouting up on rural radio, with colorful nicknames, playing the slippery, sliding guitar styles of the islands.

And, of course, the '30s was the beginning of the craze for everything cowboy. The "old West" was quickly being turned into a nostalgic land of brave, white-hatted, horseback-riding cowboys who subdued the evil Indians and outlaws who previously inhabited the land. In movies and radio, the good cowboy was always accompanied by his girl, his horse, and his guitar. Singing a romantic song as he roamed the western plains, he was the icon of an American individualist: strong, rugged, and virtuous. So, naturally, young folks emulated Roy Rogers and Gene Autry. They wanted to be cowboys, too!

Whether preserving age-old traditions or innovating new ones, it is up to the young to pass along the musical fruit of their generation. In these photos, we get a glimpse of the role that young musicians played throughout the South. Today, because most "traditional" musicians who have been "rediscovered" are older, it is important to remember that there was a time when their music was not limited to the elderly. This music spoke to the young generation just as rock, grunge, and rap do today. And because they were often far removed from record players or radios, they had to make it themselves—the original "garage" bands of the South!

A family group portrait, showing that you can't be too young to take up the fiddle! The four young fiddlers in the front row are accompanied by a single female (perhaps their sister) at the far right of the back row, holding a small single-row melodeon. The melodeon was an inexpensive, accordion-like instrument that was available through mail order or local music shops. While not usually associated with country fiddle music from Tennessee, it could have fit comfortably into the tradition. Young women were discouraged from taking up the fiddle, which was considered the "Devil's instrument." This family hailed from Tennessee, and was photographed in the teens or twenties. Photo courtesy of H. M. Slagel

Two young Hawaiians (!) from High Point, North Carolina, practice their act. Dillard Web is playing the ukulele and is posed with his cousin, Lawrence Hill, circa 1930. The white suits and leis are typical of Hawaiian-style outfits. The Hawaiian music craze swept the country from the turn of the century through the '40s; everyone wanted to play the exotic music of the islands. Ukuleles were manufactured in the thousands, many with "authentic island scenes" painted on them. Easy to play, they immediately became the amateur musician's friend. Armed with his uke, anyone could be a Hawaiian performer—at least temporarily. Photo courtesy of Leroy Hill

These local boys from Randlemen, North Carolina, played some on radio and at local theaters, when they were photographed in the mid-1930s. Part of the novelty of the act was their youthfulness, and their "western" garb (which came down to cowboy hats, if this picture is typical). Cowboys—like Hawaiians—were popularized by records, radio, and movies. The image of the cowboy survived longer than the singing Hawaiian, so even today Garth Brooks appears in a ten-gallon hat. This band's instruments are typical Sears-catalog-grade models, available readily through mail order. Back row, left to right, are: Richard Allred, Gilbert Christenberry, and Bruce Beane on guitars. Front row, left to right, are: James Hall (banjo), George Christenberry (fiddle), and Fred Allred (mandolin). Photo courtesy of the Christenberry family

*These young boys were photographed by Ben Shahn
in 1937 on the back of a truck near the square dance
at the Skyline Farms, Alabama, shown on pages
92–95. Perhaps they were satirizing the "old-style"
music that was being played by the adults; kids have
a way of viewing their parents' music as hopelessly
corny. On the other hand, many rural children took
up the challenge of preserving the traditional music of
their fathers and mothers. As far as we know, they're
just a group of kids having a good time—and music
is a part of it. The guitar appears to be an
inexpensive model with a Hawaiian scene stenciled
on the lower face.* Photo reproduced from the
Collections of the Library of Congress

The famous Cajun fiddlers Dennie McGee and Sady Courville photographed at the beginning of their long and illustrious career. Note that the fiddles are balanced on their collarbones, rather than under their chins. McGee, an orphan, was one of the greatest of all Cajun fiddlers, recording prolifically in the period of 1929–30. He was "seconded" on record by his brother-in-law, Courville, as well as fiddler Wade Frugé (who we saw on page 87 in a Mardi Gras costume). McGee also recorded with the African American accordion player Amédé Ardoin. Many decades after making their original recordings, McGee and Courville reunited to play again for various folk festivals in the '60s. Photo courtesy of Bluebird Press, Eunice, Louisiana

Olin Berrier—the fellow who owned the garage and the fancy musical instruments from pages 64–65—formed his own family band to play for local events and dances. Family bands were an extension of the idea that children helped in the family "work"— whether it was farming, coal mining, or, in this case, entertaining. Plus, the family band projected a wholesome image, and would attract family audiences—people every act wanted to draw. Note the "snakehead" Gibson A-style mandolin held by his daughter Micki. Left to right are: Olin (fiddle), Leonard (banjo), Micki, Jeanne (fiddle), and Bessie Berrier (guitar). Photographed in the summer of 1931 at the Berrier home. Photo courtesy of Jeanne Beck

The string band tradition is always said to be dying out, but then there are always young musicians who take it up again. This 1940 photo shows a group of younger and older musicians playing together at the Sutphin family home. Left to right are: Virgil Walker playing a Kay mandolin (note the asymmetrical body with its two points, a trademark of the cut-rate instrument maker), Rupert Sutphin on guitar, Norman Fry on five-string banjo, Gerald Walker also on guitar, and Sid Sutphin on fiddle. The older Sutphin holds the fiddle against the collarbone, in the old-time style. With the exception of Norman Fry, they all sport fancy, modern suits and ties. Photo courtesy of the Sutphin family

TURN YOUR RADIO ON

SMALL-TOWN AND BIG-CITY PERFORMERS

LITTLE DID THOMAS EDISON think when he sang "Mary Had a Little Lamb" into his newly invented dictation machine that he was laying the basis for an enormous entertainment industry. Similarly, when Guglielmo Marconi first experimented with long-distance radio broadcast, he was concerned with the communication of ships at sea—not with Bing Crosby's career.

Yet these pragmatic inventions would have an incredible impact on all forms of music, including rural music of the South. In the past, you would learn from the small group of musicians who lived nearby your home, which meant that small pockets of regional styles would develop based on a group of musicians, experimenting together. But now, thanks to radio and recordings, virtuoso musicians could have an influence far beyond their hometowns. The impact was immediate and incredible; where once it took decades for a new musical style to pass from hand to hand, suddenly an entire generation of musicians could be influenced by a single broadcast or recording. This is exactly what happened when Earl Scruggs first played the five-string banjo with Bill Monroe's legendary bluegrass band on the Grand Ole Opry—suddenly, everyone was playing bluegrass-styled banjo!

It is said that the country music market was discovered by accident. The recording industry was centered in the Northeast and Midwest, far from country music audiences. But when an Atlanta furniture dealer who had the concession for OKeh Records in his region asked that a local star—a fiddler and housepainter named Fiddlin' John Carson—be recorded, suddenly the northern record executives took notice. Similarly, the market for rural blues singers was only mined after urban singers—like Ma Rainey and Bessie Smith—had their success.

But once the floodgates opened, it seemed like anyone could make a record. Some were professional, some amateur, some downright surprised to be in a recording studio. But there was a market for what they did, and it was economically feasible to serve it. Music suddenly became a legitimate business, and many part-timers suddenly found themselves in full-time demand.

Local radio was also a means of establishing a soloist's or group's popularity. Fifteen-minute slots had to be filled all day long; find a sponsor, and you could have a slot. And if you wanted to use your fifteen minutes to sell songbooks or promote upcoming jobs, that was okay with the station management. Particularly during the Depression, when record sales lagged, the radio became the voice of traditional music, and a main backbone of every musician's success.

The images collected here include famous bands—like those led by Charlie Poole and Bill Monroe—and lesser-known groups. All shared in this brief renaissance of country and blues music's popularity. Many are forgotten today, but their images still speak to us of a time when radio and recordings brought a great diversity of music to every home.

Charlie Poole and his famous North Carolina Ramblers. One of the most popular performers of the late 1920s, Poole suffered—as many musicians did—from a drinking problem and died just before he would have made his Hollywood film debut in 1933. His clear singing voice, accompanied by a relatively subdued band, made his recordings immensely popular. Poole was a high liver and heavy drinker, leading to his early death, but his legendary recordings have ensured him a permanent place in the history of American country music. Many of his "hits" entered into the rural folk song repertoire. This is Poole's second recorded lineup, with fiddler Posey Rorer, Poole, and Roy Harvey photographed in 1927. Note all three are in Sunday suits. Poole holds a Gibson mastertone banjo. Photo courtesy of Kinney Rorer

Aunt Samantha Bumgarner was equally adept on fiddle, banjo, and guitar. She was among the first country-recording artists. The daughter of a fiddler, Bumgarner made her first banjo (in her words) out of "a gourd with a cat's hide stretched over it and strings made out of cotton thread waxed with beeswax." Already performing as a teenager, Bumgarner was encouraged by her husband in her musical life, which was hardly the norm for the day. In 1924 she traveled to New York with a friend, fiddler Eva Davis, to make some of the first recordings of traditional mountain banjo and fiddle music. Although she didn't record again until the folk revival of the '50s, Bumgarner remained a popular performer in her local North Carolina and at regional festivals. She was photographed here at the Asheville Folk Festival in 1937 by Ben Shahn. Note how far she holds the fiddle from her chin, resting it on her collarbone. Photo reproduced from the Collections of the Library of Congress

COL. PATTEE
"OLD SOLDIER
SEASON 1915

PIERCE   LIGGETT   COL. PATTEE   HAMERSLEY   McINT

Never Idle   *"New Act"*
"Still on The War Path"   *Working*

136

Three Boys in Blue
Two Sons of Dixie

Who actually served in opposing armies during the Civil War. Playing and singing the old-time tunes and songs "Back 'fore de war."

The Old Soldier Fiddlers on their Sixth Successful Tour of High-Class Vaudeville. Engagements in all the Leading Cities in Both United States and Canada.

Hit of the Show
Everywhere

The sole purpose the balance of our life is to make a living and to make others happy.
COL. J. A. PATTEE
Originator and Director

"Three Boys in Blue, Two Sons of Dixie." This group made a selling point out of their Civil War roots—bragging that they fought on opposite sides of the conflict. This wonderful signed calling card from circa 1915 shows how a string band—with the unusual addition of a trumpet—could make it on sheer novelty power. Imagine their stage show: "Dixie" segueing into the "Battle Hymn of the Republic." Plus all the popular songs of the day!
Photo courtesy of Jim Bollman

Photographed in the mid-1930s, Slim and Wilma Martin entertain the listeners on WALB. These kind of husband-and-wife, semiprofessional musicians would often have a fifteen-minute show on a local station (if they could find a sponsor). There usually wasn't any pay, but they could advertise other local appearances and also sell songbooks or records, if they had any. Their repertoire would typically be a mix of favorite old ballads and songs, sentimental popular hits, and hymns. Photo courtesy of Woody Greeson

Dave "Stringbean" Akeman was one of the first great country comedians, as well as a fine banjo player. He played with bands led by both Bill and Charlie Monroe. Akeman is here pictured in the guise of his alter ego, circa 1940. Along with Grandpa Jones, Stringbean was one of the most popular of the banjo-playing comedians. Combining cornpone humor with genuine instrumental talent, he carried forward the tradition of earlier performers like Uncle Dave Macon, one of the first stars of the Grand Ole Opry. The tall and lanky comedian would continue to perform through the time of his death in 1973. He and his wife were murdered in their house, leading some to speculate that thieves were looking for a stash of cash in their rural home outside of Nashville. Photo courtesy of Lance Spencer

In stark contrast to Stringbean, Gus Cannon of the Memphis String Band is dressed to the nines in this photograph taken in Memphis, Tennessee at the Hooks Brothers Studio in the late '20s. Although highly ornamented, this banjo is an inexpensive model. He is dressed in clothes suitable for a classical virtuoso. Could this have been an outfit Cannon would have worn at a typical performance? Cannon was rediscovered decades later at the beginning of the folk revival; by then, his clothing and way of life was (sadly) much reduced from his heyday.
Photo courtesy of Colin Escott, Showtime Music Archive

Here is the first of the two Robert Johnson photos we discussed in the introduction to the book. Which is the real bluesman? Take your pick! This photo-booth self-portrait, from the early 1930s, easily fits into our image of the country bluesman: cigarette hanging from his lips, rumpled shirt, rough-and-ready expression. Note the exceptionally long fingers of his hands, which gave him an unusual reach for fretting spaced chords. The singer who sang of being pursued by personal demons seemed perfectly captured in this now-tattered image. For anyone seeking a life "in the blues," this image could be a talisman. © 1989 Delta Haze Corporation. All rights reserved. Used by permission

But wait; here's the famous studio portrait of Robert Johnson, made by the Hooks Brothers Studio, one of Memphis's best photographic outfits, circa 1935. This man doesn't look like he has "a hellhound on his trail." Here the image of the rural bluesman has moved uptown. Now, he is pictured as a successful, well-dressed, and undoubtedly well-to-do performer—if only for the moment in which the picture was made. Bluesmen didn't want to look "down home"; they wanted to look modern, to project an image of worldly success. This photo does the job perfectly, although it cuts across our stereotypes of what a bluesman "should" look like.

The accordion became popular in the '30s as an accompaniment to hit songs, and found its way into cowboy-style bands as well. Here the duo is Otis and Eleanor Clements, who were members of Doc Schneider's Texans. They had their own separate radio show, cosponsored by Coca-Cola and the Verner Springs Water Company over station WFBC out of Greenville, South Carolina. They appeared at 11:45 each morning, and at 1:30 P.M. on Sundays for a half hour. Photo courtesy of Bob Carlin

WFBC was also the home to the "Hi Neighbor Boys," shown in the station's "Studio A" sometime in the mid-1930s. This is a cross section of the kind of semiamateur country acts that played on hundreds of stations throughout the South. The show, airing at 6:30 A.M. (it was important to catch farmers before they went out to work each day), featured country songs and comedy. Shown in this picture are many of the show's regulars. Their radio names are typical of the kind of "rural-sounding" names that performers took in order to appeal to their audience. Front row, left to right, are: The Hosey Brothers, "Little Zeke" (holding the Gibson guitar with the sunburst finish), the "Border Girl," Patricia Franks, Frank Caggan (holding the banjo), and Amos Garren. The second row features Jay Neas (in the cowboy hat), Doris Simpson (with the fiddle), "Sagebrush Slim" and "Scotty the Drifter" (sporting cowboy hats), and Zeb Turney (holding a Gibson J-200). The third row features the "Smilin' Troubadors" (first three in matching shirts), Texas Tex, Doc Durham (in suit), Annie Su Moon, the three Cothran Sisters, and Elizabeth Merrit. The fourth row shows four studio visitors, Smiling Glen (with mandolin), Broadus Mathis, the Woodside Trio (in the white dresses), Slim and Jimmie, and the Grant family. Photo courtesy of Bob Carlin

"FIVE ARISTOCRATIC PIGS" Compliments BALENTINE PACKING CO., Greenville, S. C.
Broadcasting Daily (Except Sunday) Over WIS, Columbia, S. C,---12:15 P. M.

*Shilling for "Balentine's 100% Pure Pork Sausage" are the "Five Aristocratic Pigs," who
broadcast daily over WIS in Columbia, South Carolina, at 12:15 P.M. Note the typical
1930s-era lineup, with accordion joining the fiddle, guitar, five-string banjo, and bass.
Bands relied on sponsors to purchase the radio time that got them on the air; great
Western Swing fiddler Bob Wills started out selling Light Crust Dough, and bluegrass
legends Lester Flatt and Earl Scruggs were famously associated with Martha White Flour.
Note the band members' stage names, given on the cardboard pigs. So, there was no
shame in being in the sausage business—as long as it facilitated great music making.*
Photo courtesy of Bob Carlin

An unknown semiprofessional band. This group combines elements of early minstrelsy—note the banjo player with the rather crude blackface on the far left—with the more modern look of cowboy-style clothing (the banjo player/comedian is wearing a cowboy hat). Country comedians were the grandchildren of the original minstrel performers; like their forbearers, they often played the banjo and took on the character of a backwoods rube, spouting bad puns and ancient jokes. The fellow on the far right was probably the radio announcer. This photo dates from the late 1920s or early 1930s. Photo courtesy of Ruth Everhart Coffey

Jay Hugh
HALL
AND HIS
HAPPY GO LUCKY BOYS

L. G.
(SHORTY)
PETERS
and His
Wash Board

HANK ANGLE
with His
BANJO

The Baby
Brother

RUFUS HALL
and Two Gun
Sheriff

Fiddling
STEVE
LEDFORD

ALL In A Nice CLEAN SHOW.   FUN FOR ALL
———————APPEARING AT———————
Oak Grove School
8 miles from Woodlawn, Va. on Hiway No. 740
Sponsored by the School
SATURDAY, NOV. 1st - 7:30 O'CLOCK P. M.

Admission: Children under 14 Years 15c. Adults 30c
(Including Federal Defense Tax)
Playing Daily Over WDBJ, Roanoke, Va.   7:15 Until 7:30 A. M. Daily

Typical advertising flyer for a country band from the 1930s. Most of these groups wanted to assure people that—despite the presence of the fiddle and banjo, associated with rowdy dance hall entertainment—what they presented was appropriate for the family. Here we see the headline: "All in a nice clean show. Fun for all." Fiddler Tommy Jarrell recalled that many dances were hardly family affairs—the men would drink heavily and many were in search of more than just a dancing partner! Fights were common. So, the importance of a "clean show— fun for all" can't be underestimated. Note also the colorful nicknames for the band members. Photo courtesy of Bob Carlin

Early in their careers, Bill and Charlie Monroe—the Monroe Brothers—appeared with announcer Byron Parker (known as "The Hired Man"), shown circa 1938. The duo was among the most popular recording acts of the '30s, featuring Charlie's relaxed lead vocals and Bill's high-tenor harmonies and lightning-fast mandolin. Both brothers combined the age-old folk traditions that they learned as children with more modern influences. Charlie picked up the popular songs, smooth stylings, and easy delivery of the popular music of the '30s and '40s, but his later bands were essentially old-fashioned. Bill went on to form his famous Blue Grass Boys, another more potent mixture of the old and new—and establish the bluegrass style of music. Photo courtesy of Bob Carlin

BILL   BYRON   CHARLIE

THE MONROE BROTHERS
AND BYRON PARKER
(THE HIRED MAN)

Gurney Thomas and His Hill Billy Pals from Asheboro, North Carolina. They recorded circa 1946 for King Records out of Cincinnati, Ohio. Note the modern instrumentation—not a banjo in sight—but three guitars, one electric lap steel (on the far right), bass, and fiddle. In the post–World War II era, country wanted to leave behind its "hayseed" image and move uptown. The semimilitaristic suits were also popular in the World War II era; Bill Monroe's early groups sported similar clothing. The honky-tonk craze was about to begin; and a new style of dance music—emphasizing bright lights, thick smoke, and loud, loud music—was soon to come into favor. Left to right are: Mitchell Parker (guitar), Gurney Thomas (guitar), Slim Martin (fiddle), Everett Moffitt (bass), Woody Greeson (guitar), and Wilburn Cranford (steel guitar). Photo courtesy of Woody Greeson

INDEX